Picasso's Childhood

In Malaga, on the 25th of October, 1881, a little boy was born. His happy parents baptized him Pablo. His complete name was Pablo Ruiz Picasso.

Early in life you could already see that he had great gifts of observation. When his father, who was an art teacher in Malaga, painted those still lifes or bouquets of flowers of which he was so fond, little Pablo didn't miss a single detail. Doves often appeared in his father's paintings, and Pablo quickly took a liking to them. mother's scissors and cu simple and so beautiful guess where his talent w

When he was ten, his father was appointed professor at the School of Fine Arts at La Coruña, and Pablo began to attend drawing classes. He soon enjoyed letting his imagination flow while he strolled around the city drawing caricatures of the different characters he met and reflecting the most anecdotical aspects of daily life.

Picasso's Adolescent Years in Barcelona

Four years later, in 1895, Picasso's father asked to be transferred again, and this time the destination was Barcelona. Thus the family could return to the Mediterranean atmosphere they had missed so much.

Shortly after their arrival in Catalonia, young Pablo told his father that he desired to enter the Llotja, the School of Fine Arts where he was a teacher. Even though the entrance exam was considered very difficult and Pablo had not yet reached the regular age of admission, he tried. To everybody's surprise, not only did he pass, but he got excellent marks.

Although the Ruiz Picasso family lived quite close to the sea and to the Llotja, Pablo was encumbered by papers and drawings, which he had to move from one place to the other. But fairly soon, when he was fifteen, his father rented a studio for him even closer to the School. In that studio, the first of many, and following a suggestion made by his father, he undertook to paint «Science and Charity». The canvas shows a physician (his father) who, in a poorly furnished room, takes the pulse of a patient (a woman who used to beg for alms near the door of his study), while a nun with a child in her arms observes the scene.

DON JOSE
TIA PEPA

«Els Quatre Gats»

After a brief stay in Madrid, at the Spanish Academy of San Fernando, and at his friend Pallarès's house in Horta de Sant Joan, to recover from a scarlet fever, Picasso returned to Barcelona, where he found his friends from the Llotja again. Somewhat distanced from his family, he entered into close contact with the people who frecuented a pub called «Els Quatre Gats», at that time the most important centre of the Art Nouveau movement in Barcelona. There he listened to the conversations of outstanding artists, like Miguel Utrillo, Santiago Rusiñol and Ramon Casas and, little by little, he discovered the latest revolutionary ideas.

In «Els Quatre Gats» he met people who were to become his life-long friends: Sabartés, Casagemas and Reventós. It was there also that he had his first exhibition —a series of portraits of fellow artists, along with other drawings.

All his friends kept talking about Paris with such great admiration that finally Picasso, caught up in their enthusiasm, decided to go there in the company of his friend Casagemas. Once in Paris, eager to learn, he spent his time observing everything with great interest; he was especially enthusiastic about the work of Toulouse-Lautrec and the music-hall atmosphere which pervaded the French capital.

This is the beginning of his so-called *«blue period»*. Probably influenced by the death of his friend Casagemas, he completely changed the subject matter of his paintings and became interested in people who suffered, who saw life through the eyes of pain and despair. He depicted them in shades of blue which gave his paintings a feeling of sadness and loneliness.

Picasso's Rose-Coloured World

Around the year 1904, Picasso finally settled down for good in Paris. At first he resided in a studio in the centre of Montmartre. Poets, painters and Bohemians shared the building with working class people like seamstresses, pedlars, etc. Together, they created a very picturesque atmosphere.

During the autumn of 1904, Picasso met Fernande Olivier, who was to become his companion until 1911. The complete change of environment, his new love and new friends helped him to overcome his depressive and rather introverted character. All this was reflected in his art; shades of rose and pink predominate in his paintings of that period and the subject matter also experienced a notable change.

During those years, Picasso often went to the circus and gradually made friends with the circus people. They liked to pose as models for this painter who showed such a great interest in their world, and Picasso was delighted with the figures of these acrobats and tightrope dancers, their bright coloured suits and their vivacious expressions.

It was, however, their more human aspects that interested Picasso above all. Very seldom did he represent them in the ring during their performances; on the contrary, they attracted him most when they were with their families, busy with their children, washing their clothes, listening to their elders, trying out new numbers, etc.

A whole world full of movement and intimacy is thus represented by Picasso with great stylization and colour harmony, in what has been called his *«rose-coloured»* period.

«Les Demoiselles d'Avignon»

He spent the summer of 1906 in Gósol, a village in the Catalan Pyrenees, and on his return to Paris he began what might be called his real pictorial revolution. From then on, his interests went beyond the purely psychological aspects of his subjects; he began to show preferences for the world of volumes and the analysis of shapes and forms. Slowly he managed to create a language of his own.

In this period he painted one of his most important works: «Les demoiselles d'Avignon». It combines aspects of arts as far removed from each other as Iberian art, Black art and the works of Cezanne. Perhaps in one of his visits to the Museum of Mankind in Paris, he discovered the sculpture of the African world which fascinated him throughout his life; and he reflected the harmonious order and the plastic purity of African art in this painting. We can also discover an influence of Iberian sculpture which, maybe, called Picasso's attention during of his stays in Madrid when he visited the Prado Museum.

These three tendencies are the seeds which allow Picasso to realize the work with which he initiated a new pictorial language known as *Cubism*.

Horta de Sant Joan and Cubism

Picasso had such happy memories of his first stay in Horta de Sant Joan in 1898 that years later, in 1909, he decided to return with his companion Fernande Olivier.

Surrounded by this rugged countryside, he was able to apply Cezanne's norm, which said that one must deal with nature through the medium of spheres, cylinders and cones. As a result, he produced a number of Cubist-style landscapes where nature appears in an assemblage of geometrical figures.

In September, he returned to Paris where he continued to put into practice the discoveries he had made in Horta de Sant Joan, applying those new procedures to portraits and still lifes.

Some years later, in 1913, Picasso introduced the technique of collage to his work; he glued pieces of newspaper, cloth, and wallpaper to his paintings. He became very fond of this new technique which allowed him to give his work a texture he had formerly been unable to achieve.

In 1916, a friend of his —the writer Jean Cocteau— convinced him to take part in the production of new decors for a Russian ballet. Thus, a new door was opened in Picasso's creative process: the world of the theatre, in which he participated on various occasions.

In 1920, his companion Olga Koklova gave birth to a son. They named him Pablo. The event produced a series of sensations in the artist that are reflected in his work. He initiated a period of great activity in which works of many different styles were produced simultaneously.

Drama in Guernica

In 1935 his marriage with Olga Koklova ended in divorce and Picasso took up a sentimental relationship with Marie-Thérèse Walter, with whom he had a daughter named Maya.

The following year, while he was in France, the Spanish Civil War broke out. Picasso, who sided with the Republicans, was appointed director of the Prado Museum.

As time went by, the news he received from Spain got worse and worse, and soon he felt the urge to help in the fight with the only weapon he had: his art. On the 27th of April, 1937, the Basque town of Guernica was bombed by the Nazis. This event, which shook the entire world, touched Picasso deeply. To express his indignation he painted the composition called «Guernica».

This work of enormous dimensions is carried out in tones of white, black and grey —colours which contribute to give an overall impression of doom and despair to the picture. In it we find mythical elements used to express the tragedy of war and oppression: the dying horse; the bull; the wounded soldier; the fleeing woman; maternity; darkness only mitigated by an oil lamp and a light bulb.

The Smoke of Vallauris

In 1947, Picasso visited a ceramics exhibition in Vallauris and there he struck up a friendship with the ceramist Georges Ramié, who offered his studio, and let him experiment with this technique which so strongly appealed to the tireless artist.

Together with Françoise Gilot, Picasso often visited Ramié's studio, where he painted happy themes from both mythological and classical sources. The atmosphere was peaceful, filled with the magic of the fire, essential for producing the ceramics. Picasso loved it and created a number of works directly related to nature.

A clear example of this moment is the «Pregnant Woman» where he again blended the reality of his life with his world of plastic arts. At that time two of his children were born from his union with Françoise —a boy, Claude, and a girl, Paloma. Picasso often drew pictures and made dolls for them which delighted them to no end.

As he gradually mastered the new technique of ceramics, the objects he produced began to lose their familiar utilitarian appearance, and new forms were created by changing the original shapes into something quite different before firing them.

The Art of Bullfighting

When Picasso went to live in La Californie, near Cannes, he renewed his contacts with the world of bullfighting. He attended the bullfights with great enthusiasm. Ever since his childhood in Malaga he had loved them —something he probably got from his father who was a great amateur.

Picasso had a very personal way of looking at that world. He always paid special attention to the fight between the different elements, the bull and the horse, the bull and man. Somehow, for Picasso, the bull was the incarnation of the strength, the violence of brutality, and the horse was the victim that never quite died, but kept fighting tenaciously.

In 1957, he finally finished a project he had begun long before the Civil War: that of illustrating the life of Pepe Hillo, a famous bullfighter in the days of Goya. Through a series of black and white smudges or blots, Picasso illustrated the different moments and movements pertaining to the art of bullfighting, and in a very special way the fight between man and animal.

«The Meninas»

While in La Californie with Jacqueline Roqué, who was to become his last wife, Picasso added an extra storey to the house. There he could enjoy wonderful peace and quiet —only interrupted by the cooing of the doves— and a full view of the Mediterranean Sea.

There, with a passion close to obsession, he dedicated himself to the interpretation of Velázquez's «Las Meninas». He did a series of 58 paintings; 48 of these are interpretations in which he reanalysed in Cubist-style Velázquez's vision of his subject.

After a month of uninterrupted work on the theme of the Meninas, he decided he needed a rest, so he began painting the doves he saw from his window. The light and the colour of the Mediterranean fill these delicately treated paintings as if he had wanted to change the stuffy atmosphere of the room of «The Meninas» for a window looking out onto the sea.

He did a last self-portrait of himself in this same manner, as if he were looking at himself before dying -event which took place on the 8th of April, 1973, in the little French village of Mougins.

The Picasso Museums

As we have seen, Picasso's relationship with Catalonia has been decisive in many moments of his life and work. He was well aware of this fact, and it was he himself who suggested to his friend Sabartés that if ever he wanted to donate his collection, he should give it to the city of Barcelona. Jaume Sabartés had been a friend and Picasso's secretary since 1935, and throughout his life he had collected the presents and donations given to him by the artist. In 1960, he reached an agreement with the city of Barcelona to create a museum which was opened to the public —uncerimoniously— in 1963. In 1970, a donation of works belonging to the family made it necessary to enlarge the museum, which today occupies three palaces along Montcada Street.

In 1985, a new museum dedicated to the works of Picasso was inaugurated in Paris, also in an old palace. As in Barcelona, people form long queues anxious to contemplate the work of this great genius of our time.